a. sweetheart

b. honey bunny

c. lovey-dovey

d. other (please specify)

....

from:

....

The Funny Thing About Love Is . . .

Written and Illustrated by

Lynn Chang

**Andrews McMeel
Publishing**

Kansas City

The Funny Thing
About Love Is . . .

Printed in China.

For information, write
Andrews McMeel Publishing, an Andrews McMeel Universal company,
4520 Main Street, Kansas City, Missouri 64111

02 03 04 05 06 RD3 10 9 8 7 6 5 4 3 2 1

ISBN 0-7407-2240-9

Library of Congress Cataloging-in-Publication Data
2001045889

This book
is dedicated
to my two loves

+

Fox

**The Funny Thing
About Love Is . . .**

You can't sleep at night but still
wake up with a

SmiLe.

Your heart does **flip-flops**

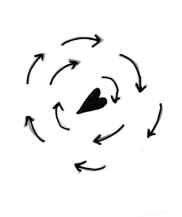

flies

Time **when you are together.**

cHOCOLATE

**no longer takes on
the importance
it once did.**

You don't care whose **TURN**

it is to call.

You both wish for the

SAME THING.

Corny love songs start taking on

GREAT
MEANING.

You get *butterflies* when you
are together.

Even really **dumb** jokes
start to make you LAUGH.

You're **ROSY** cheeked and you don't have any blush on.

You've both memorized each other's
home phone,
work phone, and cell phone
numbers and
e-mail addresses.

You actually **WANT** to share
your cookie dough ice cream.

Even a quick bite at a

local fast food restaurant seems

romantic.

EVERYTHING

seems wonderful.

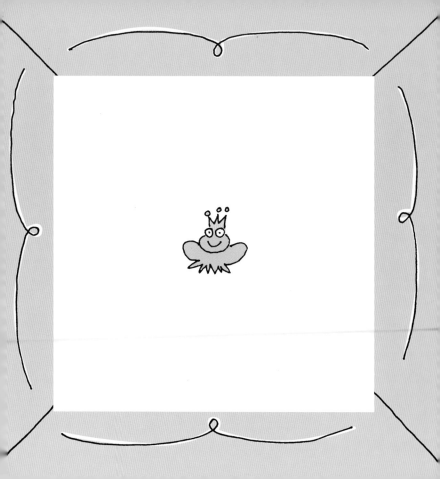

You feel LUCKY.

Stars at night seem more
sparkly.

You officially have a song called
"your song."

Without any embarrassment you wear
a T-shirt with both of you on it.

You sing **old show tunes** in the rain, without a raincoat.

You start carrying your
sweetheart's picture
in your wallet.

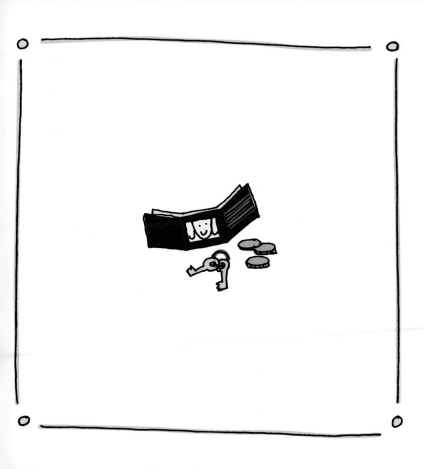

UPSIDE DOWN

You feel   and

turned
around.

You feel *swept away*

and the ocean
is a million miles away.

You **MISS YOUR EXIT**

going home.

You know **EXACTLY**

how to order your
honey bunny's coffee.

**Writing those special initials with yours
becomes your favorite doodle.**

Thinking about your lovey-dovey turns

your knees to 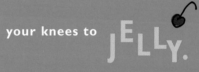JELLY.

You can't stop thinking about

your next **KISS.**

You want everyone to share the same feeling.

Being near your cutie pie sends you
to the moon.

You know why they say

love is sweet.

You're agonizing over the perfect

Valentine's Day Card

and it's November.

It **KNOCKS** you off your **feet.**

It's **HOTTER** than C^H_iL_i PE^Ppe R^S.

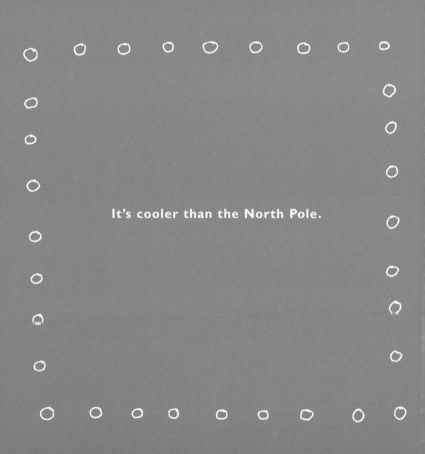

It's cooler than the North Pole.

**It's better than a king's ransom
of gold.**

It's as comforting as your ♥

TEDDY BEAR.

It makes the WORLD go round.